RACIAL JUSTICE IN AMERICA
AAPI HISTORIES

JAPANESE AMERICAN INCARCERATION

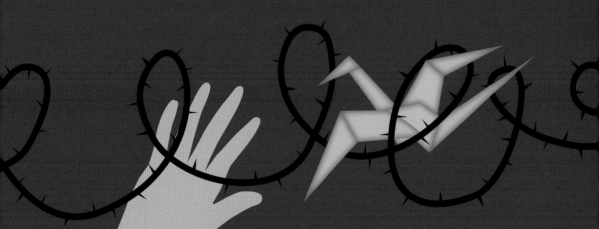

VIRGINIA LOH-HAGAN

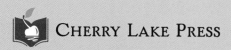
CHERRY LAKE PRESS

Published in the United States of America by Cherry Lake Publishing Group
Ann Arbor, Michigan
www.cherrylakepublishing.com

Reading Adviser: Beth Walker Gambro, MS, Ed., Reading Consultant, Yorkville, IL
Book Design and Cover Art: Felicia Macheske

Photo Credits: Library of Congress, Photo by Dorothea Lange, LOC Control No: 2021650555, 5; © Everett Collection Inc/Alamy Stock Photo, 7; Library of Congress, Photo by Esther Bubley, LOC Control No: 2017862347, 9; U.S. National Archives, Department of Defense. Department of the Army, Identifier: 12009098, 11; Library of Congress, Photo by Lee Russell, LOC Control No: 2017744876, 12; Library of Congress, Photo by Dorothea Lange, LOC Control No: 2021653171, 15; U.S. National Archives, Office for Emergency Management. Office of War Information, Identifiers: 7387536, 515297, 515295, 535645, 513871, 16; Library of Congress, Photo by Lee Russell, LOC Control No: 2017817951, 17; Library of Congress, Photo by Clem Albers, LOC Control No: 2021647285, 19;,Library of Congress, Photo by Francis Stewart, LOC Control No: 2021647202, 21; U.S. National Archives, Department of the Interior. War Relocation Authority, Identifier:537470, 23; U.S. National Archives, Commission on Wartime Relocation and Internment of Civilians, Identifier: 24746908, 25; © Simone Hogan/Shutterstock, 27; © SewCream/Shutterstock, 29

Graphics Throughout: © debra hughes/Shutterstock

Cherry Lake Press is an imprint of Cherry Lake Publishing Group.

Library of Congress Cataloging-in-Publication Data

Names: Loh-Hagan, Virginia, author.
Title: Japanese American incarceration / by Virginia Loh-Hagan.
Description: Ann Arbor, Michigan : Cherry Lake Publishing, 2022.
  | Series: Racial justice in America : AAPI histories | Includes bibliographical
  references. | Audience: Grades 4-6
Identifiers: LCCN 2022005350 | ISBN 9781668910900 (paperback)
  | ISBN 9781668909300 (hardcover) | ISBN 9781668914083 (pdf)
  | ISBN 9781668912492 (ebook)
Subjects: LCSH: Japanese Americans—Evacuation and relocation,
  1942–1945—Juvenile literature. | World War, 1939–1945—Japanese
  Americans—Juvenile literature. | Japanese Americans—Social
  conditions—20th century—Juvenile literature.
Classification: LCC D769.8.A6 L65 2022 | DDC
  940.53089/956073—dc23/eng/20220228
LC record available at https://lccn.loc.gov/2022005350

Cherry Lake Publishing Group would like to acknowledge the work of the Partnership for 21st Century Learning, a Network of Battelle for Kids. Please visit http://www.battelleforkids.org/networks/p21 for more information.

Printed in the United States of America

Dr. Virginia Loh-Hagan is an author, former K-8 teacher, curriculum designer, and university professor. She's currently the Director of the Asian Pacific Islander Desi American (APIDA) Center at San Diego State University. She is also the Co-Executive Director of the Asian American Education Project. She identifies as Chinese American and is committed to amplifying APIDA communities.

CHAPTER 1

What Is the Japanese American Incarceration Experience?

During World War II (1939–1945), the United States was at war with Japan. More than 120,000 Japanese Americans were forcefully removed from their homes. From 1942 to 1945, they were sent to incarceration sites. The U.S. government called the sites "relocation camps," but they were prisons.

Japanese Americans were rounded up and sent far away from their homes. They were stripped of their rights and treated like criminals. Their lives were uprooted and destroyed. They had to sell or give away their property, lands, and businesses. Many families were separated. Japanese American Incarceration was a dehumanizing experience.

For some Japanese American families, White friends and neighbors would take care of their homes and businesses while they were incarcerated.

Japanese American Incarceration was a huge injustice that is unknown to some people. It's important to learn about what happened so it never happens again. It's also important to use the correct words to honor the experience. Those who were incarcerated may use whatever words they choose. They can describe their own experiences.

"Incarceration" is a better word than "imprisonment." It describes people being detained unfairly. A person is imprisoned when guilty of a crime. But a person can be incarcerated for different reasons. Incarcerated means to be confined. It does not always mean guilt.

"Internment" has been used to describe this experience too. It refers to detaining enemy soldiers. The Japanese American Incarceration detained our own citizens, not foreigners. So, Japanese Americans weren't interned. They were incarcerated.

Think About It! Many Japanese Americans burned anything they had from Japan. They wanted to avoid being accused of disloyalty. How would you feel about burning important family possessions? How would you feel about having to hide your culture and past?

Some people are incarcerated for standing up for social justice. For example, Dr. Martin Luther King Jr. was incarcerated almost 30 times. He fought for civil rights.

DID YOU KNOW...?

Many people use words in specific ways. They want to justify their actions. The U.S. government did this when they referred to the removal of Japanese Americans as an "evacuation." This word means being saved from a natural disaster. It also means being moved for protection. Japanese Americans were not evacuated. They were removed, expelled, or excluded. Aiko Herzig-Yoshinaga was an activist. She wanted those that were incarcerated to receive justice. She knew the importance of using words. She said, "Words can lie or clarify." Language can distort the truth. Use words that accurately describe what happened.

CHAPTER 2

What Is the History of the Japanese American Incarceration Experience?

The United States has a history of discriminating against Asian Americans. This hate against Asians can be traced back to "Yellow Peril." Yellow Peril is the fear of rising Asian power. It's the belief that Asian countries are going to take over Europe and the United States. White people feared being invaded and enslaved.

In the 1930s, Japan grew into a world power. It wanted to expand. It conquered lands in China and other parts of Asia. In 1940, Japan entered World War II. It signed an agreement with Germany and Italy. The three countries formed a military alliance called the Axis powers. They agreed to support each other if attacked. They agreed that Germany and Italy would have control over Europe and that Japan would have control over East Asia.

The United States was closest to Japan. It was the only nation capable of fighting against the Japanese. At first, the United States refused to enter the war. It didn't want to interfere in the affairs of Europe and Asia. That all changed on December 7, 1941, when Pearl Harbor Naval Base in Hawai'i was attacked.

Newspapers of the time promoted the idea of Yellow Peril. The media has always been a powerful force in spreading ideas.

Japan wanted to be the dominant power in the Pacific. It wanted to build its military. It needed oil for military tanks and ships. It attacked countries in Asia to get their oil. It wanted to stop the United States from defending these countries. It aimed to destroy U.S. military power. So, it attacked Pearl Harbor. President Franklin D. Roosevelt described the date as one "which will live in infamy . . ."

Japanese submarines fired torpedoes at the base. Japanese planes dropped bombs. Japan's attack lasted 1 hour and 15 minutes. The Japanese sank or damaged more than 18 U.S. Navy ships and destroyed more than 300 U.S. planes. More than 2,400 Americans died, and nearly 1,200 people were hurt.

The United States was taken by surprise. It couldn't let the attack go unpunished. Americans were ready to fight. The next day, the United States declared war on Japan. It entered World War II.

 Think About It! Some experts don't think the Pearl Harbor attack was a surprise. They think the United States wanted to be seen as victims of Japanese violence to enter the war. Research this. What role do you think the United States played in the war with Japan?

DID YOU KNOW...?

Manjiro was the first Japanese immigrant to come to the United States. He arrived on a whaling ship in 1843. The 14-year-old fisherman was caught in a storm. His ship and crew washed up on a deserted island, 300 miles (482 kilometers) away from Japan. Five months later, Manjiro and his crew were rescued by William Whitfield. Whitfield captained a U.S. whaling ship. He adopted Manjiro, renaming him John Mung. Manjiro lived in Massachusetts and later returned to Japan. He became a samurai, then an ambassador between Japan and the United States. Twenty years later, Japanese immigrants arrived in Hawaiʻi to work in the sugarcane fields. From there, they migrated to the West Coast. Then many more Japanese people came to the United States.

At the time, many Americans accused Japanese Americans of being spies. There was no proof of this. On February 19, 1942, Roosevelt passed Executive Order 9066. This law targeted "enemy aliens." It allowed for their forced removal and incarceration. It did not specifically mention Japanese Americans. But Japanese Americans were most affected by it.

The fear was that Japan had easy access to the West Coast. The law affected people from areas "deemed vulnerable to attack or sabotage." This meant people living within 100 miles (97 km) of the West Coast.

On March 29, 1942, Public Proclamation No. 4 was issued. It was authorized by Executive Order 9066. The forced removal and incarceration of Japanese Americans on the West Coast began. Japanese Americans were given 48 hours to pack.

CHAPTER 3

Why Were Japanese Americans Incarcerated?

After the bombing of Pearl Harbor, people looked for a scapegoat. Japanese Americans were an easy target. They looked like the enemy. They were blamed. They were accused of being Japanese spies.

In addition to incarceration, other swift actions were taken against Japanese Americans. Their bank accounts were frozen. They were banned from owning guns or radios. They weren't allowed to be in public between 8:00 p.m. and 6:00 a.m.

Their rights were taken away in many ways. This was all justified as a "military necessity." National security was seen as more important than civil rights.

Think About It! There were racist laws against the Japanese community. For example, Japanese Americans couldn't marry outside of their race. Why did such laws exist? What other groups suffered under racist laws?

NOTICE

Citizens were encouraged to report any suspicious behaviors. This led to racist people making false reports about Japanese Americans.

REMEMBER PEARL HARBOR.....WORK~FIGHT~SACRIFICE!!

"Remember Pearl Harbor" was a slogan used to rally public support for the war. It was also used to support anti-Japanese efforts.

DID YOU KNOW...?

To prove their loyalty, many incarcerated Japanese Americans joined the military. They served in all branches. About 33,000 Japanese Americans served during World War II. The 442nd Infantry Regiment was an all-Japanese American unit. It formed in 1943. Its motto was "Go For Broke." It was the most decorated unit in U.S. military history. The 442nd soldiers rescued a Texas National Guard unit that was trapped deep in a forest in France and surrounded by 6,000 German troops.

Japanese Americans were seen as "perpetual foreigners." This stereotype was a basis for Japanese American Incarceration. It allowed Japanese Americans to be seen as "the other." It positioned them as different, exotic, and foreign. It's rooted in xenophobia. During this time, Japanese Americans weren't seen as Americans but as dangerous foreigners.

Before the Pearl Harbor attack, there was growing racism against the Japanese community. Japanese Americans were achieving successes. They were farmers and business owners. This threatened White Americans' jobs. The Pearl Harbor attack gave many in the the United States a reason to act on their racism.

Some people benefited from the Japanese American Incarceration. They claimed lands and property that didn't belong to them.

CHAPTER 4

What Happened at the Japanese American Incarceration Camps?

After being rounded up, Japanese Americans were taken to temporary holding places. The government called these places assembly centers. Shelters were quickly built on fairgrounds and racetracks. Japanese Americans were forced to live in animal stalls.

After about 3 to 6 months, Japanese Americans were sent to incarceration camps. These camps were located many miles inland. They were in remote and bleak places. There were 10 camps. Two camps were in California at Manzanar and Tule Lake. Two camps were in Arizona at Gila River and Poston. Two camps were in Arkansas at Jerome and Rohwer. Idaho had a camp in Minidoka. Utah had a camp at Topaz. Wyoming had a camp at Heart Mountain. Colorado had a camp at Granada. Today, many of these sites are museums.

At the camps, many families were crowded together. They shared barracks, bathrooms, and dining rooms. They had very little privacy and no freedom. They faced poor living conditions. They had little or no medical care. Guard towers and barbed wire surrounded the camps. People who tried to escape were shot.

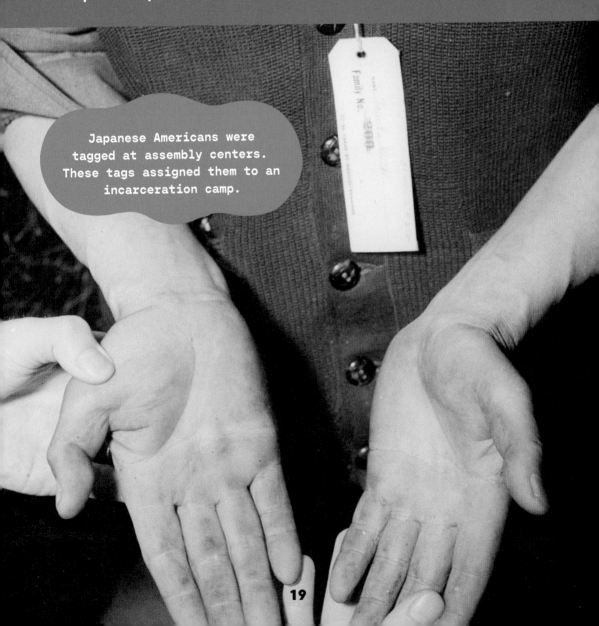

Japanese Americans were tagged at assembly centers. These tags assigned them to an incarceration camp.

Japanese Americans were forced to live in these camps for years. For many, survival was their way of resisting. Many Japanese Americans tried to make the best of it. They embodied *shikata ga nai*. This Japanese phrase means "it cannot be helped." They created their own communities, schools, and gardens. They hosted concerts. They made art to improve their living spaces.

Some Japanese Americans found ways to fight back. Minoru Yasui, Gordon Hirabayashi, and Fred Korematsu were involved in famous court cases. They claimed the incarceration was illegal. Some Japanese Americans hosted protests, strikes, and riots.

Think About It! Many incarcerated Japanese Americans did not trust the government. When they were asked to fill out a government questionnaire about their loyalty to the United States, they thought it was a trick. How would you feel about being questioned about your loyalty? Look up the questions. How would you answer them?

Many incarcerated Japanese Americans used whatever supplies they could find to make things they needed. For example, they made their own furniture out of scraps.

DID YOU KNOW...?

The U.S. government hired six photographers to document the Japanese American Incarceration. Dorothea Lange was the first one hired. She documented the removal process. Ansel Adams was given permission to photograph Manzanar. On the other hand, the U.S. government banned incarcerated Japanese Americans from having cameras. David Tatsuno and Toyo Miyatake had hidden cameras while incarcerated. Their footage provided records of what happened from the perspective of those incarcerated. Some of the incarcerated Japanese Americans were professional artists. Mine Okubo painted and drew to document her experiences. She mailed her works to friends outside of the camps. She wanted to "tell the story of camp life."

CHAPTER 5

What Happened after the Japanese American Incarceration Experience?

Incarcerated Japanese Americans suffered greatly. They faced shock, shame, fear, uncertainty, helplessness, and more. After World War II ended, they were released from the camps. Life was hard for them. Many had lost their homes, jobs, and businesses. They had to start over. They also had to deal with a country that didn't want them. Racist groups actively worked to exclude them.

Some Japanese Americans didn't like to talk about the incarceration. They kept their feelings to themselves. They felt silenced by the trauma. But other Japanese Americans didn't want to keep silent. They saw the incarceration as a racial injustice and an attack on their American identity.

Activists from the Japanese American Citizens League and other groups have been fighting for reparations.

They want money to make up for lost time and profits. They also want people to care and not let this happen again. They fought to be remembered. On February 19, 1978, the first Day of Remembrance in Washington state was observed.

After release, some incarcerated Japanese Americans moved back to their hometowns. Some moved to different towns.

On February 19, 1976, President Gerald Ford said, "February 19th is the anniversary of a sad day in American history." He referred to the signing of Executive Order 9066. He signed a law formally ending it. He added, "...Japanese Americans were and are loyal Americans."

In 1980, the U.S. Congress created the Commission on Wartime Relocation and Internment of Civilians. This group investigated the Japanese American Incarceration experience. More than 750 people testified. The commission wrote a report called "Personal Justice Denied." It described the incarceration as a "grave injustice." It denied the military necessity of incarceration.

The commission's report led to the Civil Liberties Act of 1988. This act was signed into law by President Ronald Reagan. Reagan issued a public apology. In addition, the law gave money to surviving incarcerated Japanese Americans. It stated that government actions were based on "race prejudice, war hysteria, and a failure of political leadership."

Think About It! The U.S government referred to the process of Japanese Americans being released as "resettlement." It wanted to resettle these Americans into the middle of the country. Why would the U.S. government might want to avoid the development of "Japantowns" on the West Coast?

DID YOU KNOW...?

Plans for moving Japanese Americans out of the camps started in 1942. The National Japanese American Student Relocation Council (NJASRC) was formed. It worked with many groups. It placed incarcerated Japanese Americans in colleges. By the end of World War II, about 4,300 Japanese Americans were placed. Japanese Americans were sent to more than 600 colleges in the Midwest and on the East Coast. They endured being separated from their families. They worked to create positive images about Japanese Americans. NJASRC raised tuition money. It also built community support to ensure new, positive experiences. Despite this, some Japanese American students faced racism at their colleges.

CHAPTER 6

What Is Still Happening Today?

Today's immigration issues have similarities to the Japanese American Incarceration experience. Fears against immigration are related to national security. Some Americans think immigrants will take away their jobs or use up our nation's resources.

The United States continues to use detention as a solution. It has the largest immigration detention system in the world. The U.S. Immigration and Customs Enforcement (ICE) is in charge of the detention and deportation process. It conducts raids and rounds up migrants. It investigates migrants. It holds migrants at detention centers. These detention centers are located all over the country. They're often overcrowded. They don't have enough food or supplies. Migrants are detained there for weeks or months.

Like with Japanese American Incarceration, families are separated. In 2018, President Donald Trump's policies separated more than 2,300 U.S.-born children from their parents. This happened at the Mexico-United States border. The parents were deported to their countries of birth. These issues point at problems with detention and racist policies.

Border states like Texas and California have the most detention centers.

Think About It! Like with the Japanese Americans, people of color continue to serve as scapegoats for our nation's problems. One example is Asian Americans being blamed for the COVID-19 pandemic. What are some other examples of communities being scapegoats? Have you ever been blamed for something you didn't do? How did it make you feel??

The Japanese American Incarceration also helped contribute to the "Model Minority Myth." After their incarceration ended, many Japanese Americans did not want to be seen as threats. They feared being rounded up again. So, they led quiet, lawful lives. They wanted to be accepted. They worked hard to fit in.

This led to sociologist William Peterson's article in *The New York Times Magazine* in 1966. The article was titled "Success Story: Japanese American Style." Peterson celebrated Japanese Americans. He called them "model minorities." He said they rose from incarceration to high levels of accomplishment. He said they did so by not being angry or resentful like other groups. He praised them for not using state programs like public assistance. He referred to other communities of color as "problem minorities."

The Model Minority Myth suggests that Asian Americans are better than other minorities. This thinking is racist. It pits Asian Americans against other minorities. Racist policies and laws became more targeted at Black and Mexican Americans. Communities of color should strive to work together to fight for racial justice.

Not all Asian American groups are achieving success. Some are struggling. They need money and resources. But they are neglected because they are seen as model Americans.

DID YOU KNOW...?

On September 11, 2001, terrorists from the Middle East attacked the United States. Some Americans wanted to ban Arab Americans and Muslims from all flights. Some wanted to round them up and detain them. Norman Mineta was U.S. Secretary of Transportation at that time. During World War II, he was incarcerated at Heart Mountain. After the 9/11 attack, Mineta met with President George W. Bush to share his experiences. Bush said, "We want to make sure that what happened to [Mineta] in 1942 doesn't happen today." Mineta emailed major airlines. He warned against targeting or discriminating against people. He didn't want others to be incarcerated the way he was.

SHOW WHAT YOU KNOW!

The Japanese American Incarceration was a major injustice. Let's work to never let this happen again.

Research what life was like at the incarceration camps. Japanese Americans were mistreated there. But they also built strong communities. Some continue to visit the camps. They host reunions there.

Show what you know! Choose one or more of these activities:

- Interview someone who was incarcerated at the camps or is a descendant. Write a report about how the incarceration affects their lives today.

- Visit one of the incarceration camps. Create a brochure for the camp. Share the history and how Japanese Americans were treated. Share ways to support the preservation of the history.

- Study images about the Japanese American Incarceration. Compare and contrast the differences between images by those incarcerated versus those approved by the government.

- Read all the books in the *Racial Justice in America* series. Create a journal, podcast, or social media campaign. Include a segment about the Japanese American Incarceration.

 Think About It! Think about all the things you have learned. What would you like to learn more about?

SHOW WHAT YOU CAN DO!

Share your learning. Being an ally is the first step in racial justice work. Allies recognize their privilege. We all come from different positions of privilege. We also have different types of privilege. In the United States, being White is a privilege. Other examples include being male or an English speaker.

Use your privileges. Use it to help all achieve equality. Japanese American Incarceration taught us that targeting people is unfair. Here are ways you can be an ally:

- Seek other solutions besides detention. Learn ways to improve policing to benefit people of color. Talk to others about what it means to defund the police.

- Don't blame groups of people for hardships. Examine systems instead.

- Speak out if you see someone being targeted.

We all have a role to play in racial injustice. We also have a role in making a better world. Do your part. Commit to racial justice!

Think About It! Think about your privileges. Do you want to improve the lives of others? What are you willing to give up to do this?

EXTEND YOUR LEARNING

NONFICTION

Knutson, Julie. *Born in 1919: Fred Korematsu and Jackie Robinson*. Ann Arbor, MI: Cherry Lake Publishing, 2020.

Loh-Hagan, Virginia. *A Date Which Will Live In Infamy: Attack on Pearl Harbor*. Ann Arbor, MI: Cherry Lake Publishing, 2019.

Loh-Hagan, Virginia. *A is for Asian American: An Asian Pacific Islander Desi American Alphabet Book*. Ann Arbor, MI: Sleeping Bear Press, 2022.

Loh-Hagan, Virginia. *Citizens Imprisoned: Japanese Internment Camps*. Ann Arbor, MI: Cherry Lake Publishing, 2020.

Public Broadcasting Service: Asian Americans
https://www.pbs.org/weta/asian-americans

GLOSSARY

aliens (AY-lee-uhnz) people who live in a country and are not citizens of that country

alliance (uh-LYE-uhns) an agreement to work together

ally (AH-lye) a person who is aware of their privilege and supports oppressed communities

barracks (BEHR-uhks) buildings where soldiers or detainees live for a short amount of time

commission (kuh-MIH-shuhn) a group of people chosen to perform a certain task

defund (dee-FUHND) to withdraw funding from

dehumanizing (dee-HYOO-muh-nyz-ing) depriving of human qualities or dignity

deportation (dee-por-TAY-shuhn) the forced removal of someone from a country

descendant (dih-SEHN-duhnt) a member of the future generation of people

executive order (ig-ZEH-kyoo-tiv OR-duhr) a rule or order made by the U.S. president

hysteria (hih-STEHR-ee-uh) very strong or unmanageable emotion

incarceration (in-kahr-suh-RAY-shuhn) confinement

infamy (IN-fuh-mee) evil or shameful reputation

migrants (MYE-gruhntz) people who go from one place to another, especially to find work

pandemic (pan-DEH-mik) an epidemic spread over multiple countries or continents

peril (PEHR-uhl) danger

perpetual (puhr-PEH-chuh-wuhl) never-ending

privilege (PRIV-lij) a special, unearned right or advantage given to a chosen person or group

proclamation (prah-kluh-MAY-shuhn) an official announcement

public assistance (PUHB-lik uh-SIS-tuhns) aid in the form of money or necessities for people in need

reparations (reh-puh-RAY-shuhnz) acts or processes of making amends for wrongdoing or injury

sabotage (SAH-buh-taj) to secretly destroy or damage something

scapegoat (SKAYP-goht) a person who is unfairly blamed for something that others have done

sociologist (soh-see-AH-luh-jist) a person who studies human societies or groups

testified (TEH-stuh-fyed) gave evidence

torpedoes (tor-PEE-dohs) missiles used to destroy ships

vulnerable (VUHL-nuh-ruh-buhl) open to attack or damage

xenophobia (zeh-nuh-FOH-bee-uh) the fear or dislike of people from other countries.